My Sight Word List

a	in	said
and	is	see
away	it	the
big	jump	three
blue	little	to
can	look	two
come	make	up
down	me	we
find	my	where
for	not	yellow
funny	one	you
go	day	
help	play	
here	red	
I	run	

Name: ___________________ Date: ___________

Today is: Monday | Tuesday | Wednesday | Thursday | Friday

Direction: Trace and read the sentences.

fun	gun	run	sun
आनंद	बंदूक	daud	रवि

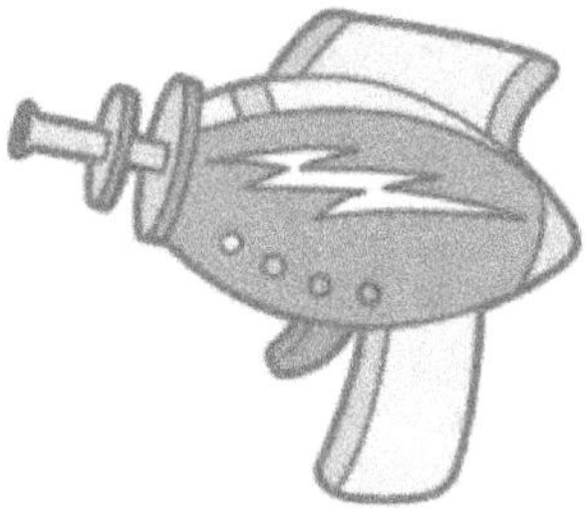

They are having fun.

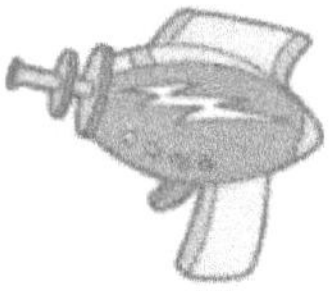

He has a gun.

The bear is running.

The sun is smiling.

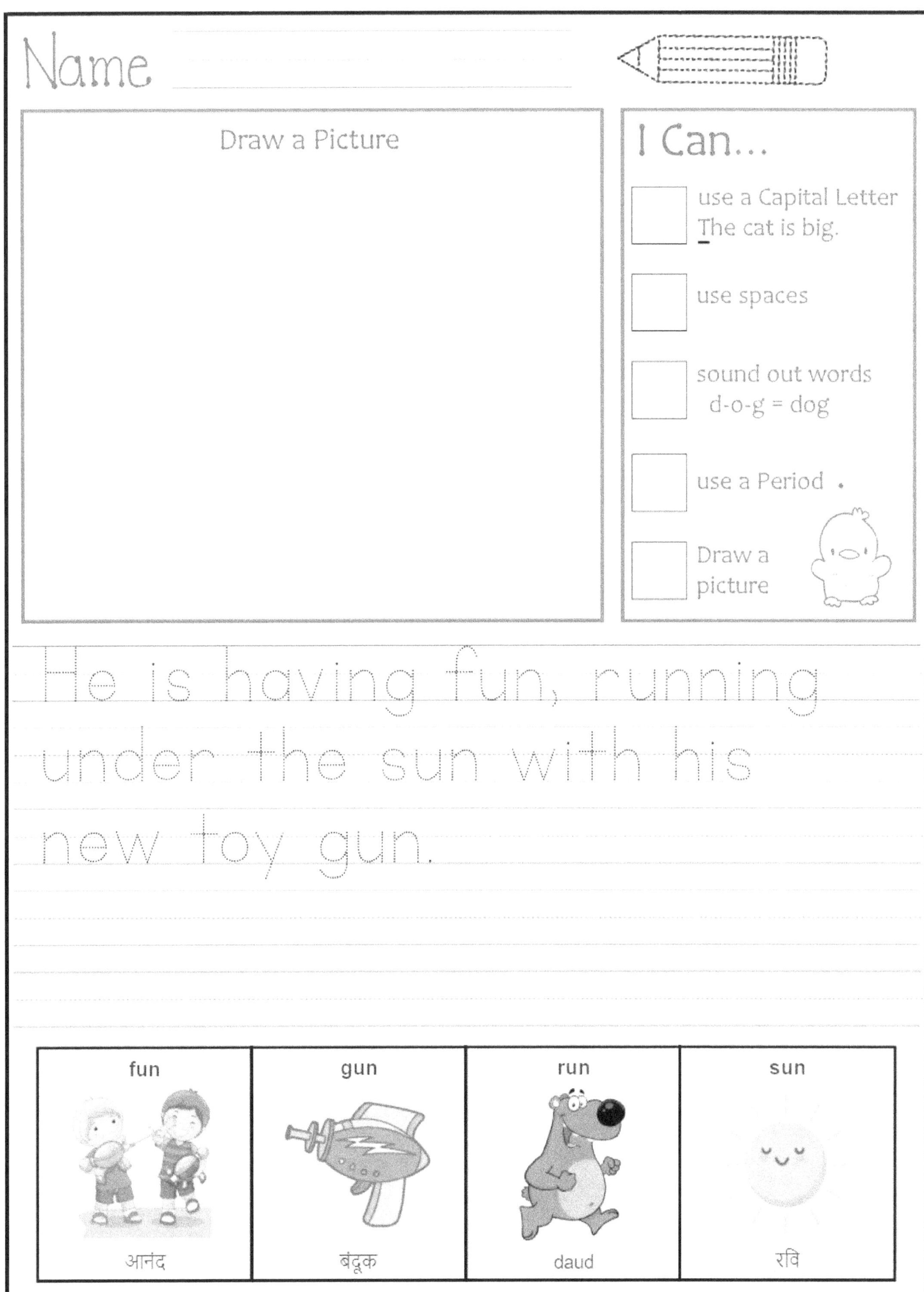

Name

Draw a Picture

I Can...

use a Capital Letter
The cat is big.

use spaces

sound out words
d-o-g = dog

use a Period .

Draw a
picture

He is having fun, running
under the sun with his
new toy gun.

fun
आनंद

gun
बंदूक

run
daud

sun
रवि

Name: ______________________ Date: ______________________

Today is: Monday | Tuesday | Wednesday | Thursday | Friday

Direction: Trace and read the sentences.

bag	rag	tag	wag

बैग	खपरैल	टैग	wagging

He has many bags.

I see a rag.

I see a tag.

Its tail is wagging.

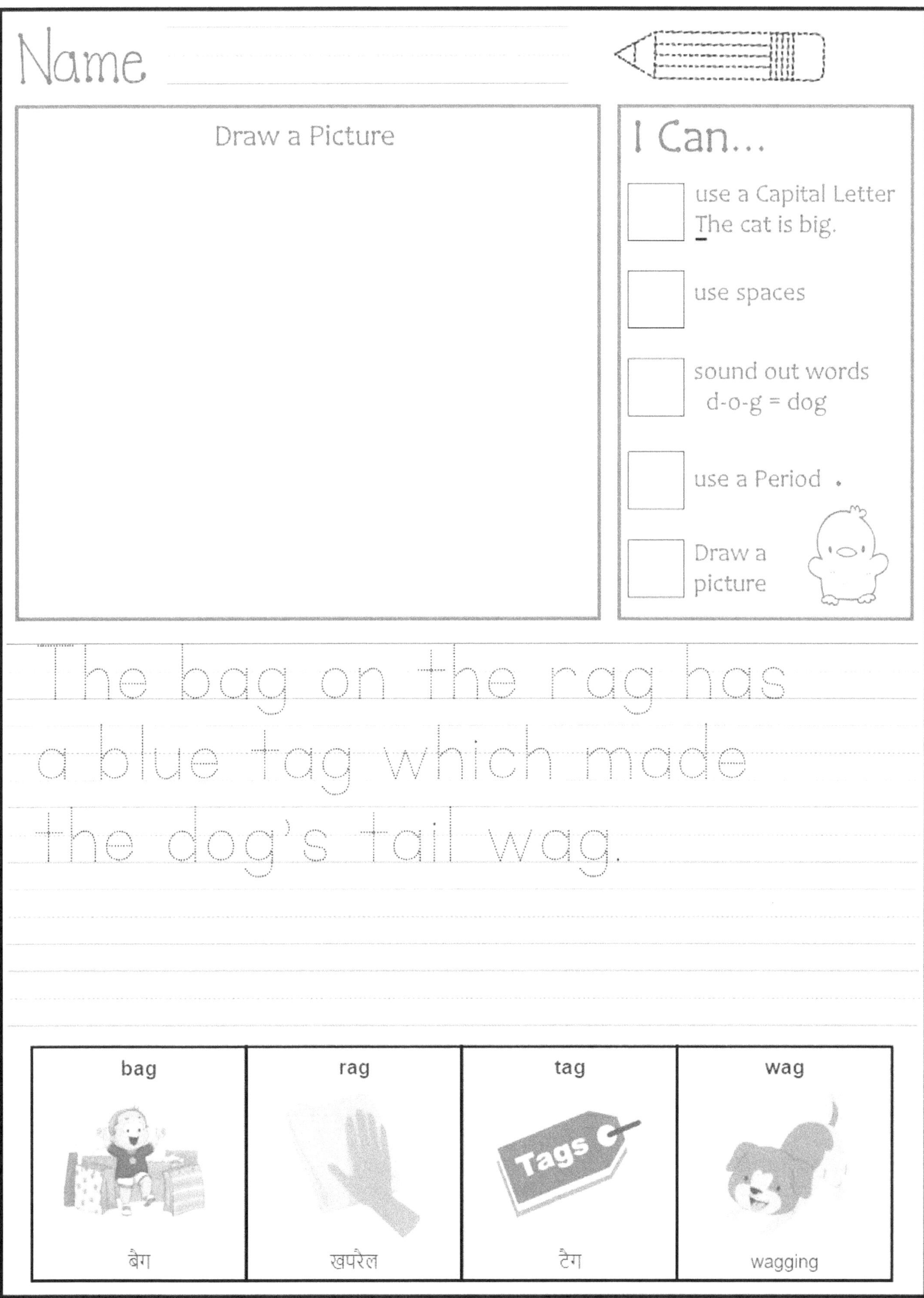

Name

Draw a Picture

I Can...

use a Capital Letter
The cat is big.

use spaces

sound out words
d-o-g = dog

use a Period .

Draw a
picture

The bag on the rag has
a blue tag which made
the dog's tail wag.

bag
बैग

rag
खपरैल

tag
टैग

wag
wagging

Name: ____________________ Date: ____________________

Today is: Monday Tuesday Wednesday Thursday Friday

Direction: Trace and read the sentences.

can	man	pan	van

डिब्बे	आदमी	कड़ाही	वैन

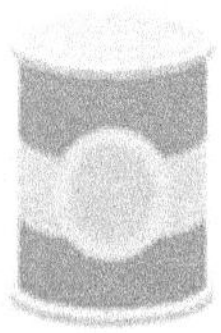 I see a can of soda.

 The man is happy.

 The pan is dirty.

 I see a big van.

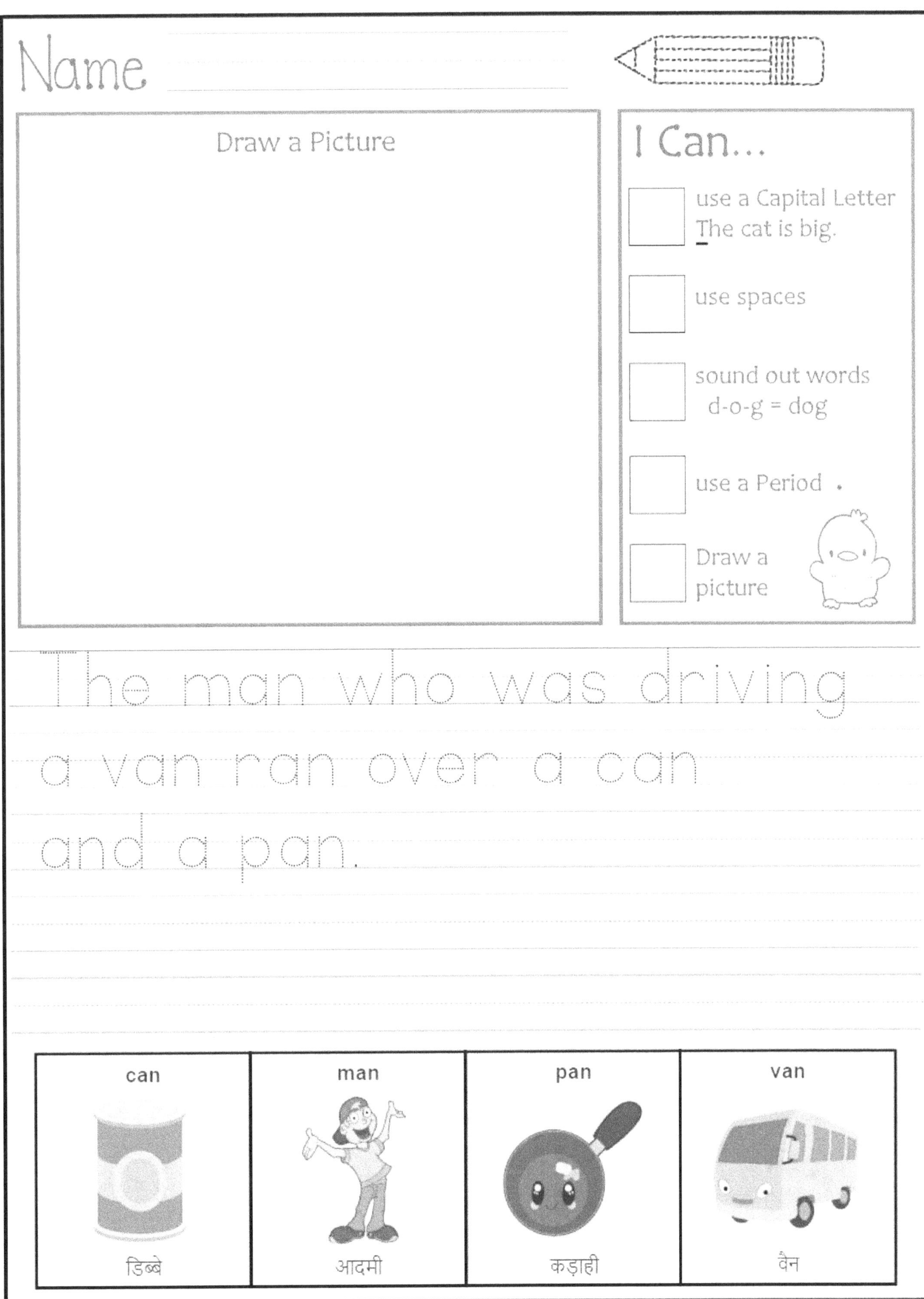

Name

Draw a Picture

I Can...

use a Capital Letter
The cat is big.

use spaces

sound out words
d-o-g = dog

use a Period .

Draw a
picture

The man who was driving
a van ran over a can
and a pan.

can
डिब्बे

man
आदमी

pan
कड़ाही

van
वैन

Name: ______________________ Date: ______________________

Today is: Monday Tuesday Wednesday Thursday Friday

Direction: Trace and read the sentences.

cut	gut	hut	nut

कट गया	आंत	कुटिया	अखरोट

He cut his nails.

He has a gut.

This is a small hut.

It is holding a nut.

Name _______________________

Draw a Picture

I Can...

- ☐ use a Capital Letter
  The cat is big.
- ☐ use spaces
- ☐ sound out words
  d-o-g = dog
- ☐ use a Period .
- ☐ Draw a picture

cut	gut	hut	nut
कट गया	आंत	कुटिया	अखरोट

Name: ____________________ Date: ____________________

Today is: Monday Tuesday Wednesday Thursday Friday

Direction: Trace and read the sentences.

fat	cat	hat	mat

मोटी	बिल्ली	टोपी	चटाई

I see a fat dog.

This is my little cat.

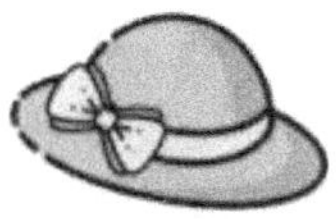

I like this hat.

I see a big mat.

Draw a Picture

I Can...

- [ ] use a Capital Letter
  The cat is big.
- [ ] use spaces
- [ ] sound out words
  d-o-g = dog
- [ ] use a Period .
- [ ] Draw a picture

The fat cat laid on the mat that was a hat pattern.

fat	cat	hat	mat
मोटी	बिल्ली	टोपी	चटाई

Name: ____________________ Date: ____________________

Today is: Monday | Tuesday | Wednesday | Thursday | Friday

Direction: Trace and read the sentences.

cab	lab	tab	crab

टैक्सी	प्रयोगशाला	टैब	केकड़ा

The cab is fast.

The lab is exciting.

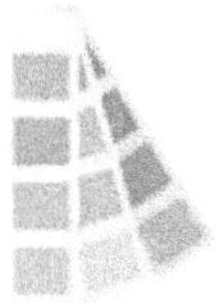

The tab is long.

We found a crab.

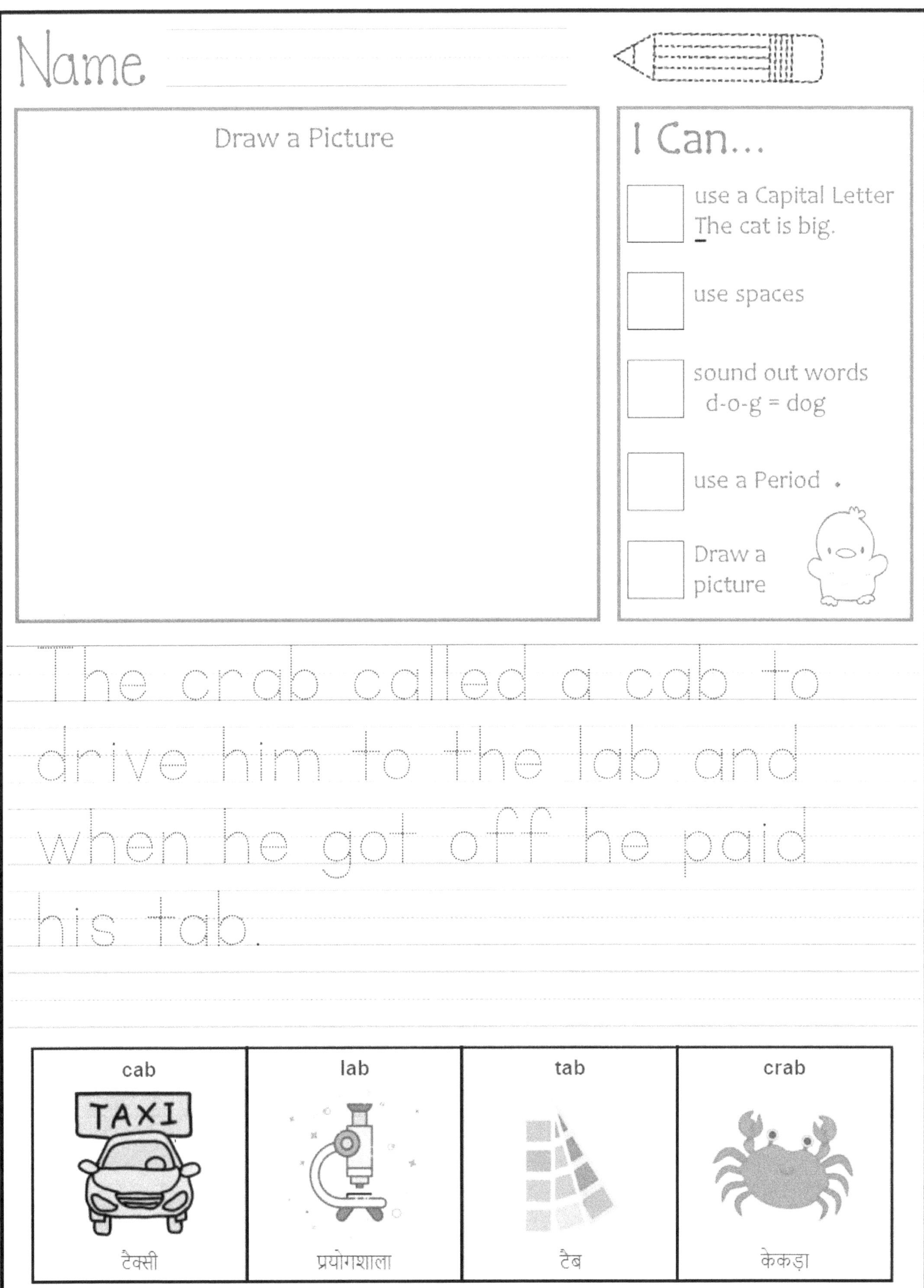

Name

Draw a Picture

I Can...

use a Capital Letter
The cat is big.

use spaces

sound out words
d-o-g = dog

use a Period .

Draw a
picture

The crab called a cab to
drive him to the lab and
when he got off he paid
his tab.

cab
TAXI
टैक्सी

lab
प्रयोगशाला

tab
टैब

crab
केकड़ा

Name: _________________ Date: _________

Today is: [Monday] [Tuesday] [Wednesday]
[Thursday] [Friday]

Direction: Trace and read the sentences.

ham	jam	ram	clam
जांघ	जाम	भेड़	खोल

I like to eat ham.

We like to eat jam.

The ram is big.

The clam is pretty.

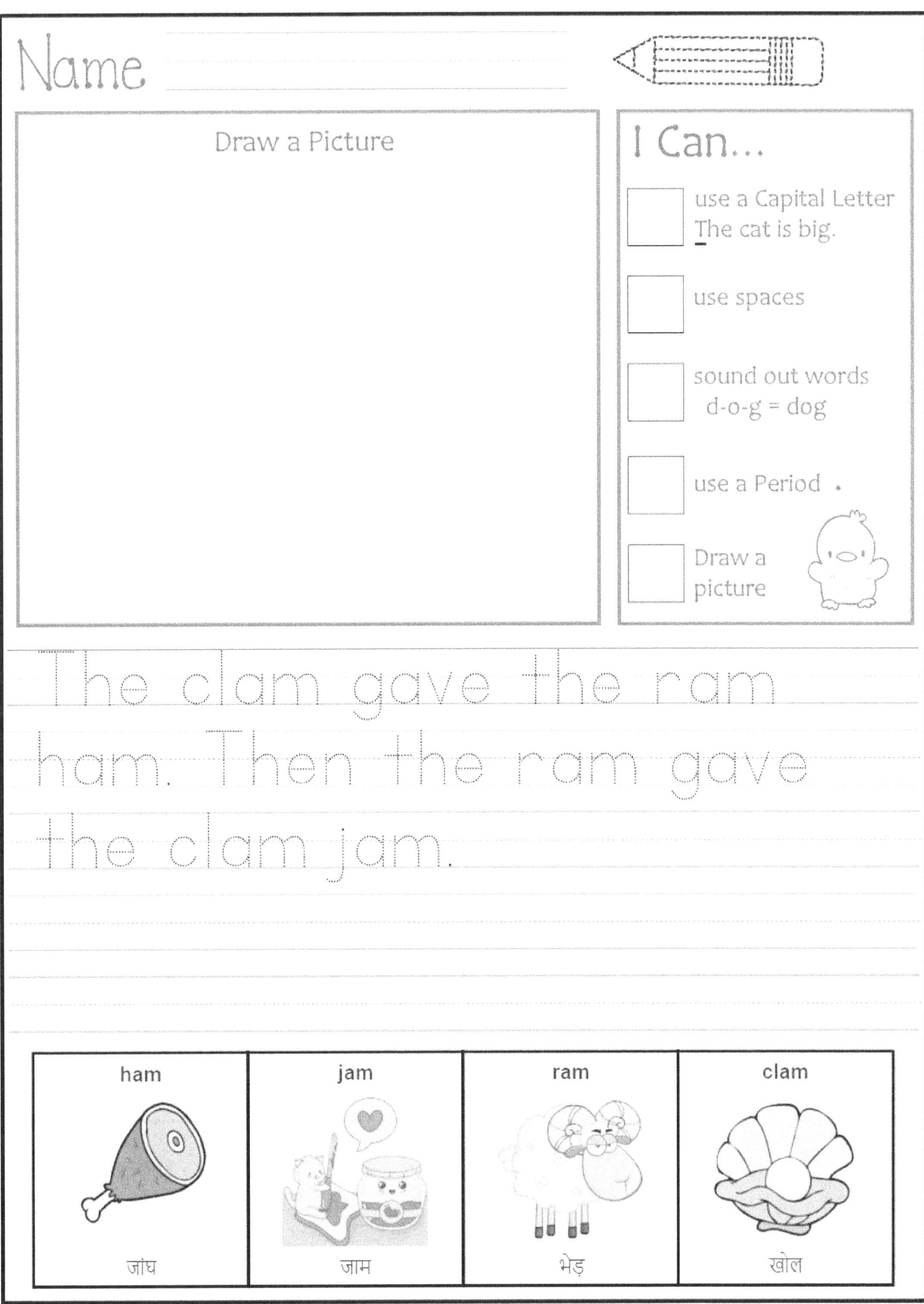

Name

Draw a Picture

I Can...

use a Capital Letter
The cat is big.

use spaces

sound out words
d-o-g = dog

use a Period .

Draw a
picture

The clam gave the ram
ham. Then the ram gave
the clam jam.

ham
जांघ

jam
जाम

ram
भेड़

clam
खोल

Name: ______________________ Date: ______________________

Today is: Monday Tuesday Wednesday Thursday Friday

Direction: Trace and read the sentences.

bed	led	red	wed
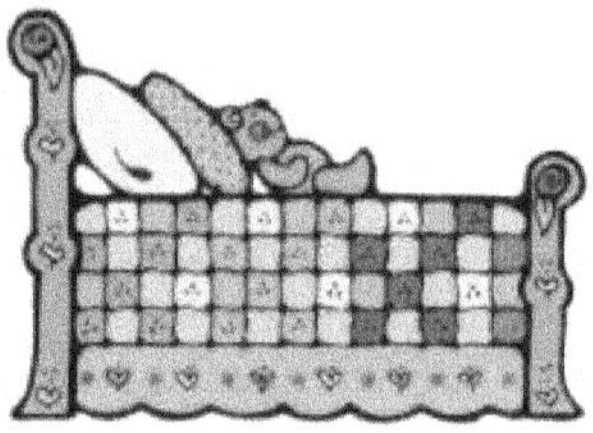			
बिस्तर	प्रमुख	लाल	शादी

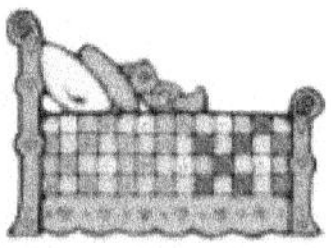

This is my little bed.

He led us to safety.

The apple is red.

He asks her to wed.

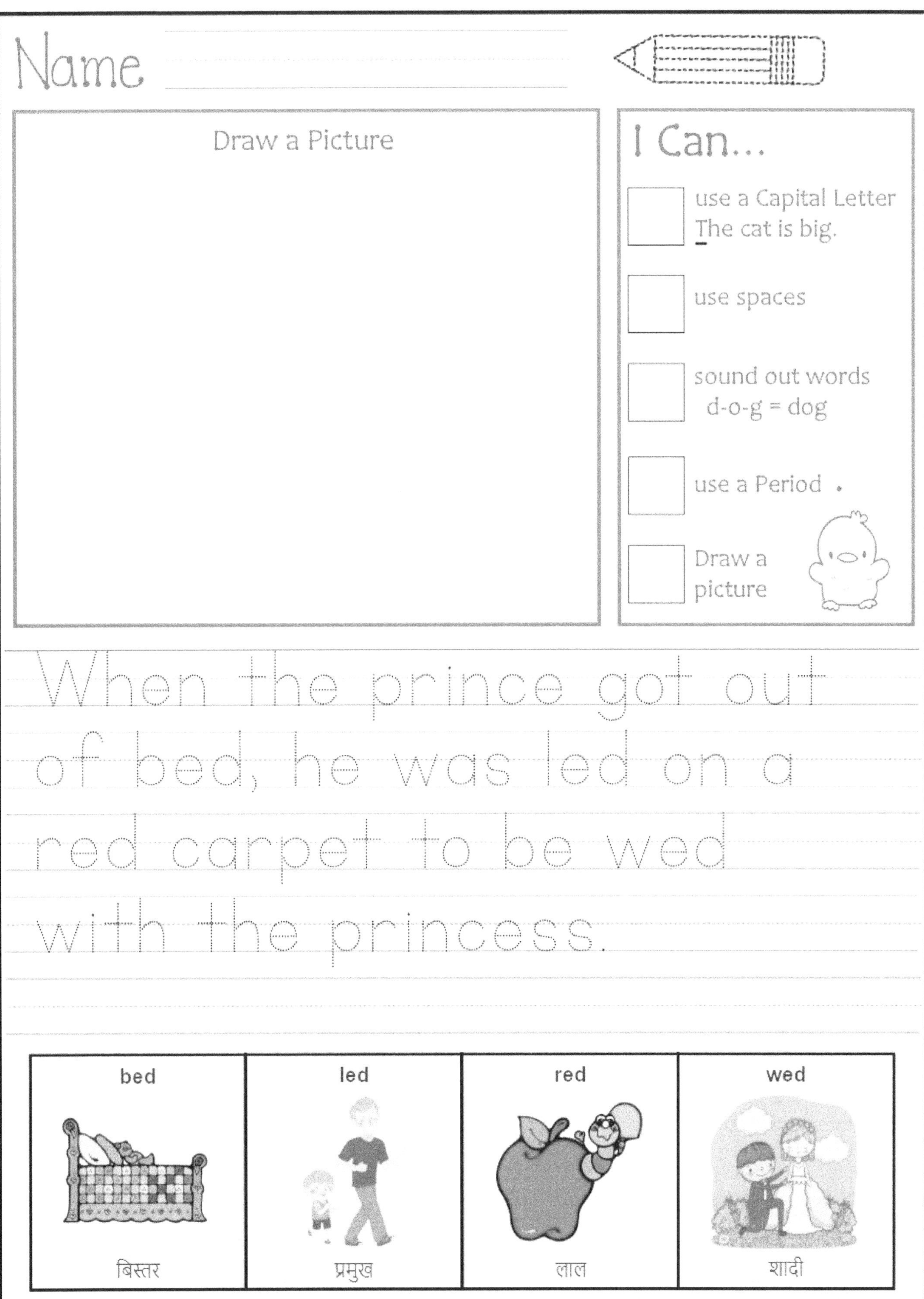

Name
Draw a Picture
I Can...
use a Capital Letter
The cat is big.
use spaces
sound out words
d-o-g = dog
use a Period .
Draw a picture
When the prince got out of bed, he was led on a red carpet to be wed with the princess.
bed
led
red
wed
बिस्तर
प्रमुख
लाल
शादी

Name: _______________ Date: _______

Today is:
[Monday] [Tuesday] [Wednesday]
[Thursday] [Friday]

Direction: Trace and read the sentences.

bad	dad	mad	sad
खराब	पिता	पागल	उदास

This apple is bad.

My dad is very kind.

The reindeer is mad.

The little cat is sad.

I was bad so my dad
got mad and now
I am so sad.

bad	dad	mad	sad
खराब	पिता	पागल	उदास

Name: ___________________ Date: ___________

Today is: Monday Tuesday Wednesday Thursday Friday

Direction: Trace and read the sentences.

den	hen	pen	ten
मांद	मुर्गी	अस्तबल	दस

It is a den.

The hens lay eggs.

She has a good pen.

The ten is smiling.

Draw a Picture

I Can...

- [ ] use a Capital Letter
  The cat is big.
- [ ] use spaces
- [ ] sound out words
  d-o-g = dog
- [ ] use a Period .
- [ ] Draw a picture

The hen that lived in the
pen laid ten eggs
in her den.

den	hen	pen	ten
माद	मुर्गी	अस्तबल	दस

Name: _________________ Date: _______

Today is: Monday | Tuesday | Wednesday

Thursday | Friday

Direction: Trace and read the sentences.

gum	mum	sum	drum
चिपचिपा	मां	योग	ड्रम

I like to chew gum.

My mum is kind!

I can do a sum!

The drum is big.

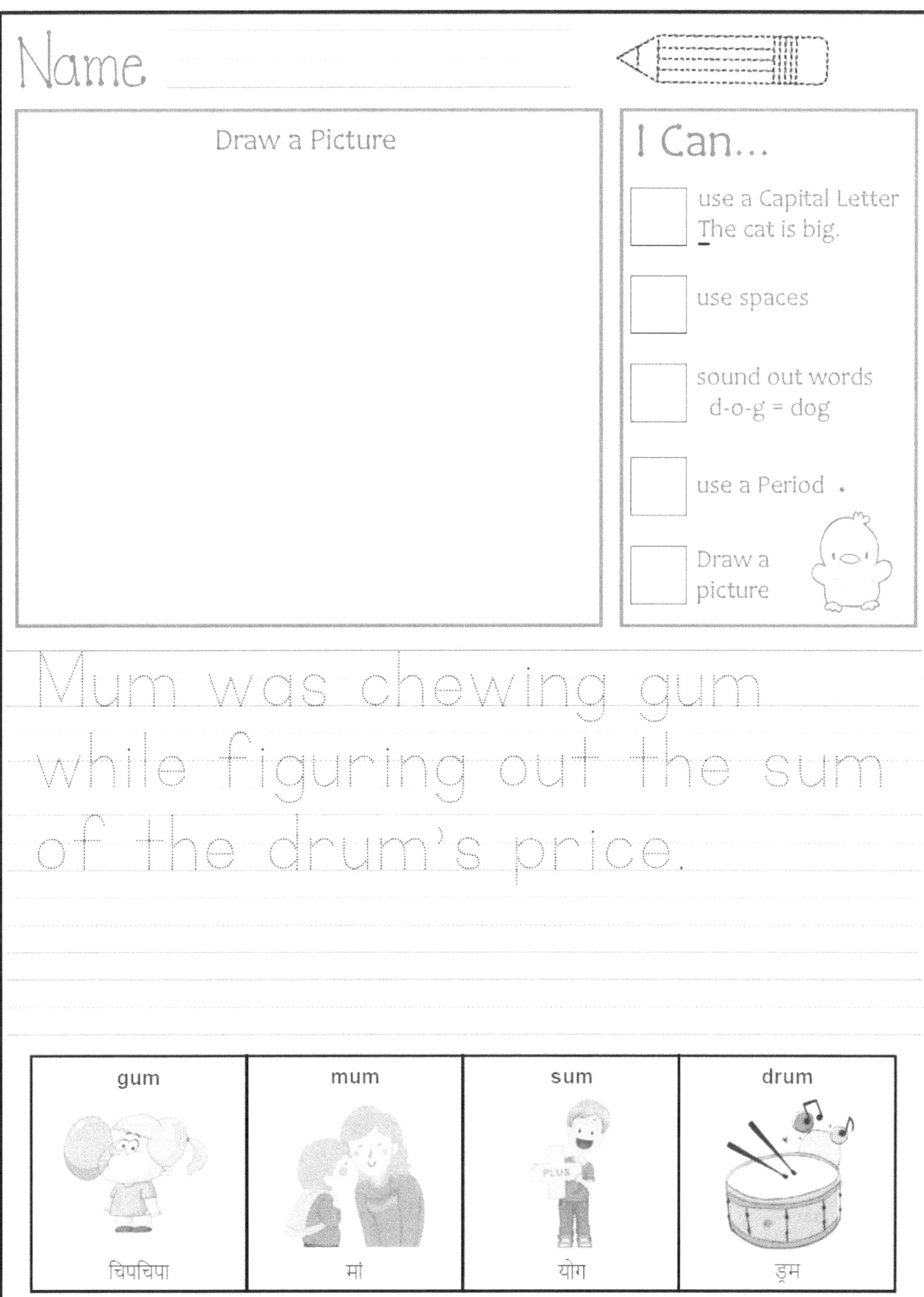

Name

Draw a Picture

I Can...

use a Capital Letter
The cat is big.

use spaces

sound out words
d-o-g = dog

use a Period .

Draw a
picture

Mum was chewing gum while figuring out the sum of the drum's price.

gum
चिपचिपा

mum
मां

sum
योग

drum
ड्रम

Name: ____________________ Date: ____________________

Today is: Monday Tuesday Wednesday Thursday Friday

Direction: Trace and read the sentences.

bid	hid	kid	lid
			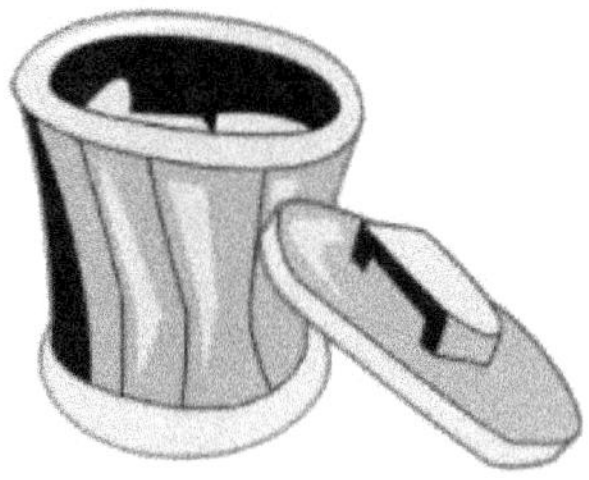
बोली	छिपाना	बच्चा	ढक्कन

He likes to bid.

He is hiding.

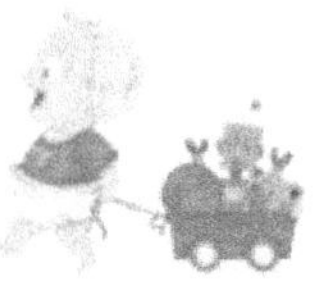

The kid like to play.

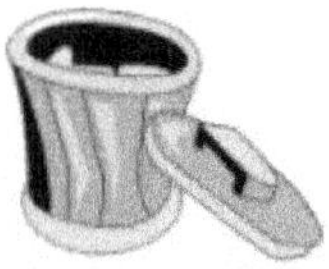

I see a lid.

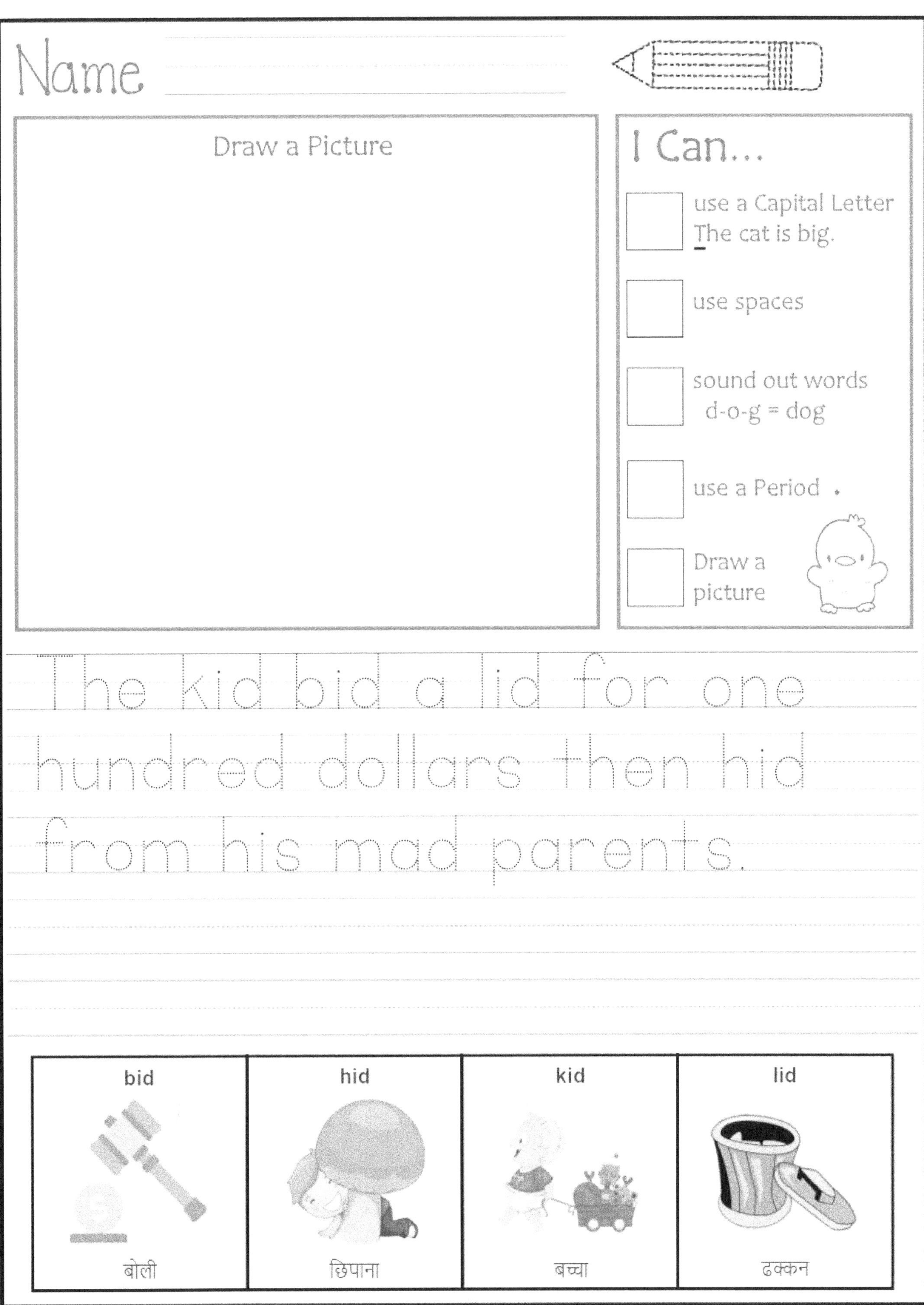

Name

Draw a Picture

I Can...

use a Capital Letter
The cat is big.

use spaces

sound out words
d-o-g = dog

use a Period .

Draw a picture

The kid bid a lid for one hundred dollars then hid from his mad parents.

bid
बोली

hid
छिपाना

kid
बच्चा

lid
ढक्कन

Name: _______________ Date: _______________

Today is: Monday | Tuesday | Wednesday | Thursday | Friday

Direction: Trace and read the sentences.

big	dig	pig	wig
बड़े	गड्ढा करना	सूअर	विग

That is a big pencil.

He will dig up a hole.

The pig is fat.

She puts on a wig.

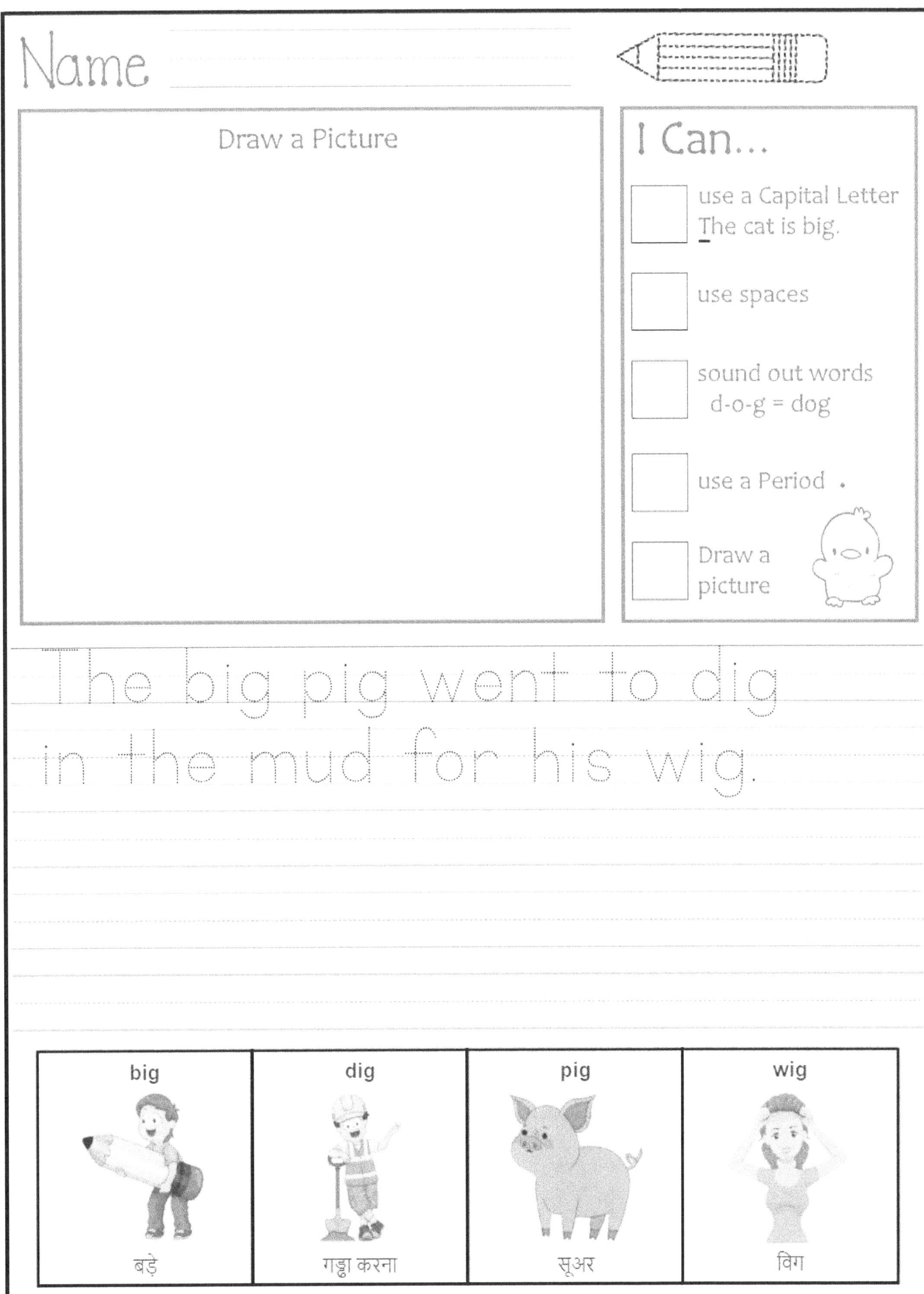

Name

Draw a Picture

I Can...

use a Capital Letter
The cat is big.

use spaces

sound out words
d-o-g = dog

use a Period .

Draw a
picture

The big pig went to dig
in the mud for his wig.

big
बड़े

dig
गड्ढा करना

pig
सूअर

wig
विग

Name: _________________ Date: _______________

Today is: [Monday] [Tuesday] [Wednesday]
[Thursday] [Friday]

Direction: Trace and read the sentences.

bin	fin	pin	win
बिन	पंख	पिन	जीत

It is a recycle bin.

The shark has a fin.

The pin is pointy.

He won the match.

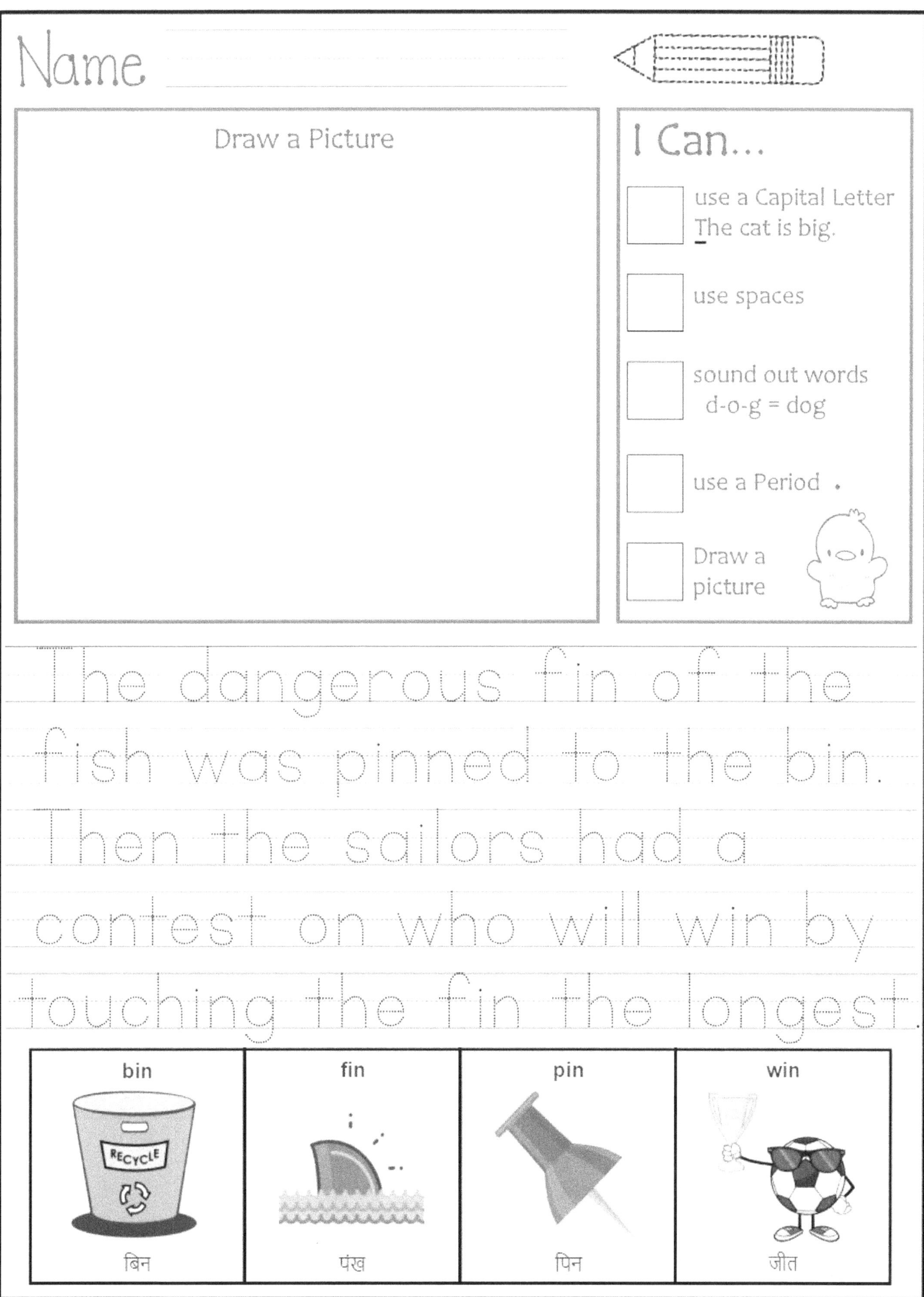
Name

Draw a Picture

I Can...

use a Capital Letter
The cat is big.

use spaces

sound out words
d-o-g = dog

use a Period .

Draw a
picture

The dangerous fin of the
fish was pinned to the bin.
Then the sailors had a
contest on who will win by
touching the fin the longest.

bin
RECYCLE
बिन

fin
पंख

pin
पिन

win
जीत

Name: ______________________ Date: ______________________

Today is: Monday Tuesday Wednesday Thursday Friday

Direction: Trace and read the sentences.

hip	lip	nip	sip

कमर	होंठ	चुटकी	पीना

This is my hip.

Her lips are red.

It is nipping its toy.

She is sipping.

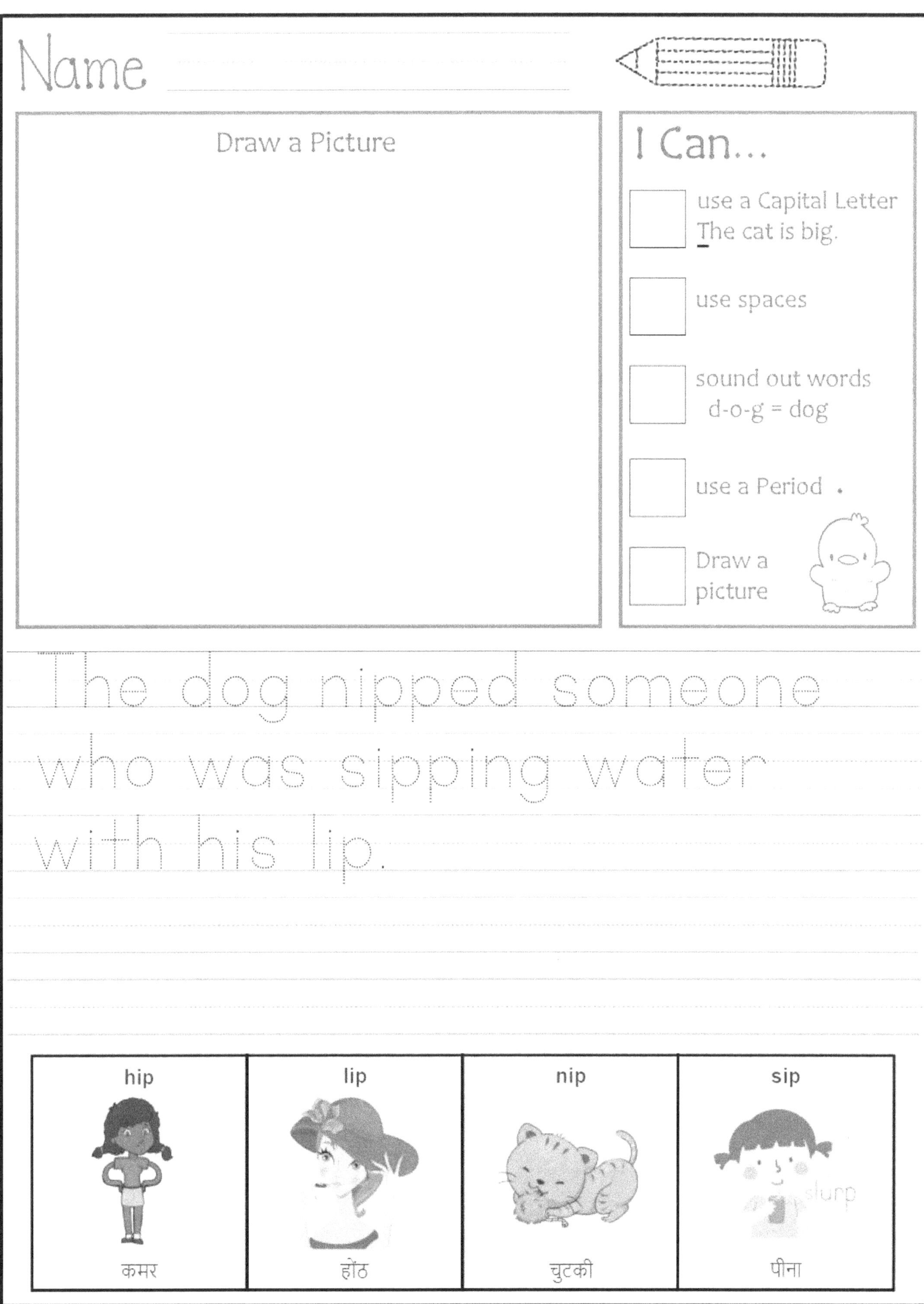

Name

Draw a Picture

I Can...
use a Capital Letter
The cat is big.

use spaces

sound out words
d-o-g = dog

use a Period .

Draw a
picture

The dog nipped someone
who was sipping water
with his lip.

hip
कमर

lip
होंठ

nip
चुटकी

sip
पीना

Name: ________________________ Date: ____________

Today is: Monday | Tuesday | Wednesday
Thursday | Friday

Direction: Trace and read the sentences.

fit	hit	kit	sit
फिट	मारो	किट	बैठिये

It is perfectly fit.

They hit each other.

That is a safety kit.

He is sitting.

The fit doctor sat then
was hit by a kit.

fit	hit	kit	sit
फिट	मारो	किट	बैठिये

Name: _______________ Date: _______

Today is: Monday | Tuesday | Wednesday
Thursday | Friday

Direction: Trace and read the sentences.

cob	job	rob	sob
मक्का	काम	लूटना	रोना

I ate corn on the cob.

This is my job.

He is robbing.

The girl is sobbing.

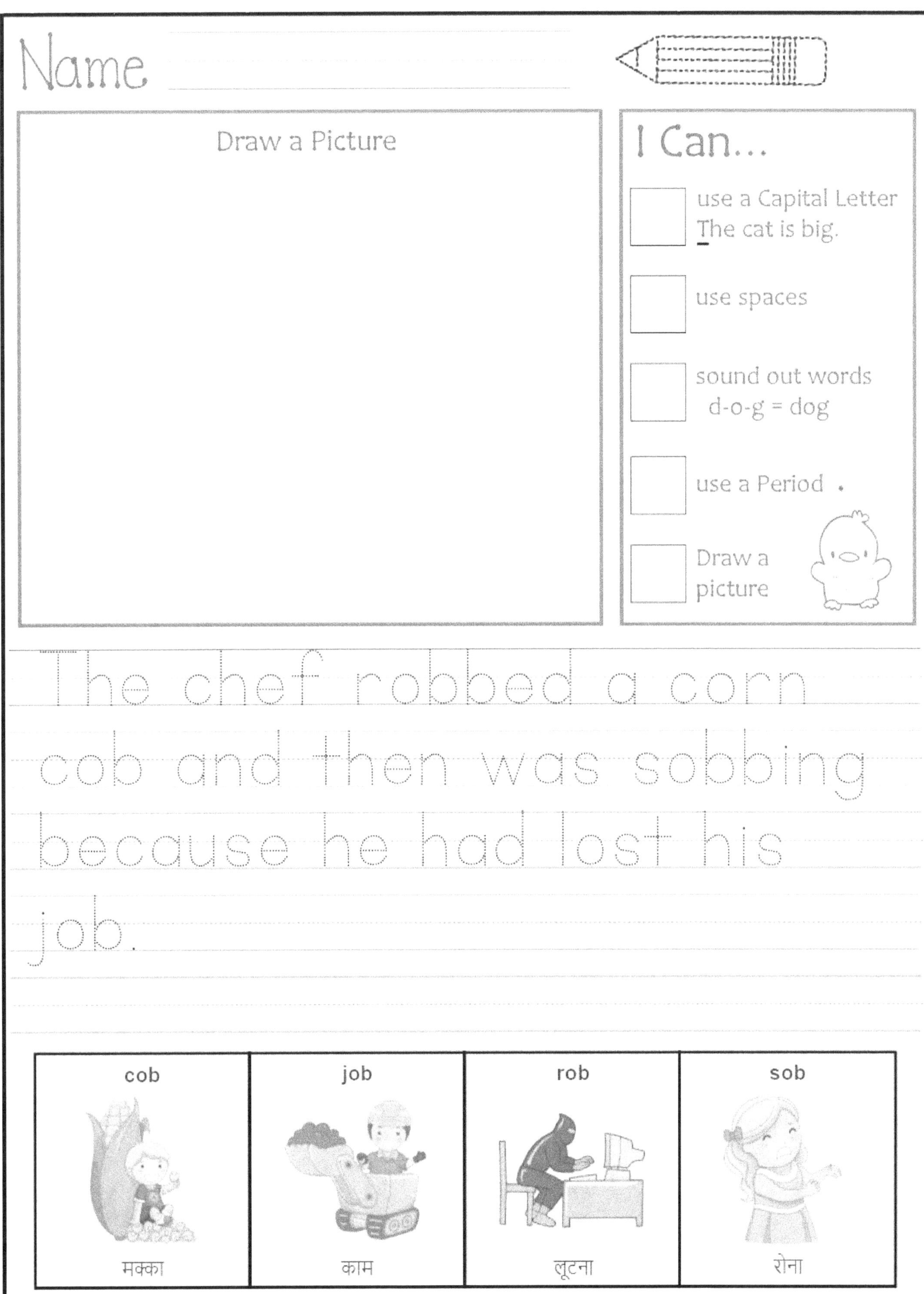

Name

Draw a Picture

I Can...

use a Capital Letter
The cat is big.

use spaces

sound out words
d-o-g = dog

use a Period .

Draw a
picture

The chef robbed a corn
cob and then was sobbing
because he had lost his
job.

cob
मक्का

job
काम

rob
लूटना

sob
रोना

Name: ___________________ Date: ___________

Today is: [Monday] [Tuesday] [Wednesday]
[Thursday] [Friday]

Direction: Trace and read the sentences.

dog	hog	jog	log
कुत्ता	सूअर	जॉगिंग	लकड़ी

The dog is thrilled.

The hog is big.

She is jogging.

The log is small.

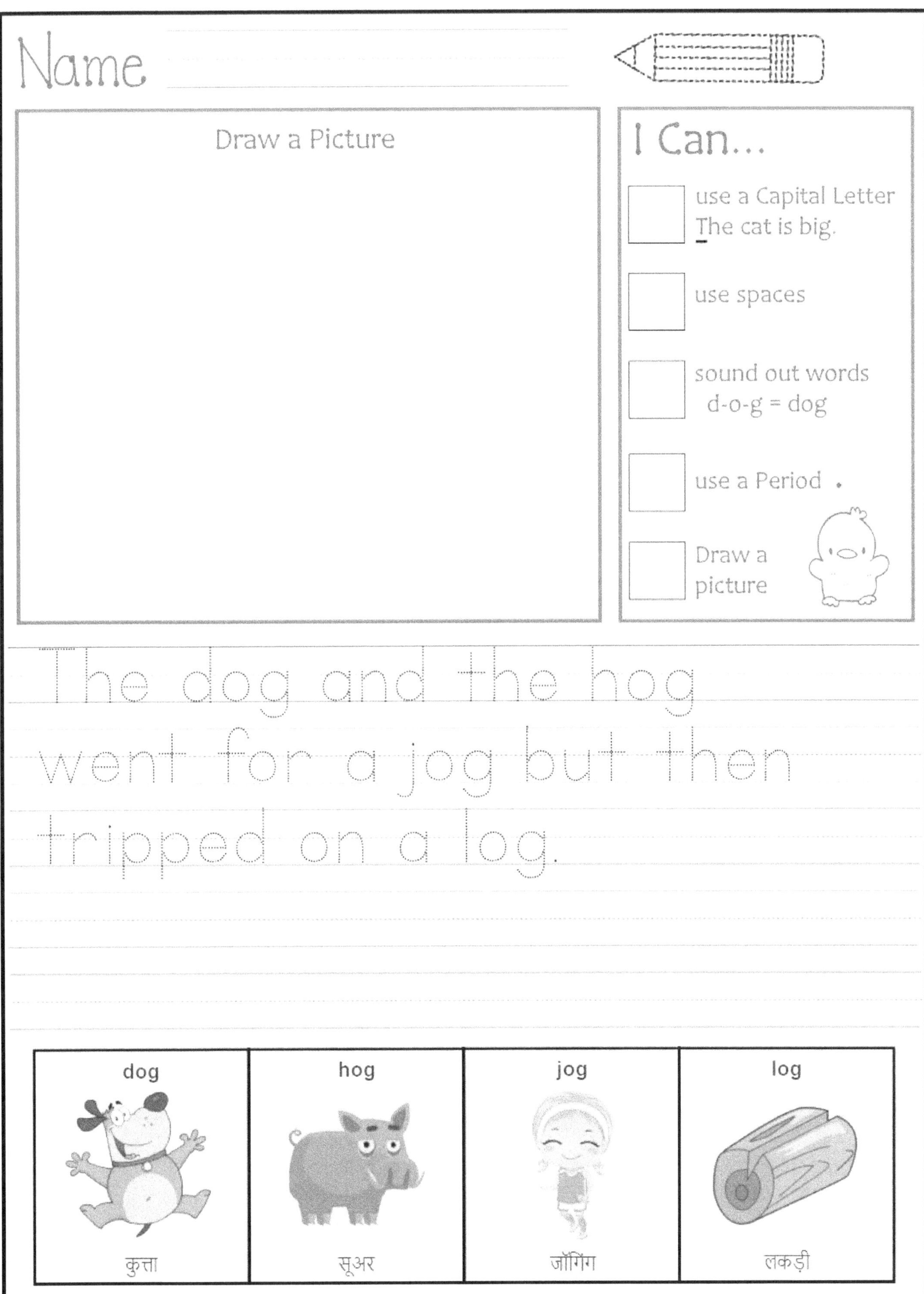

Name
Draw a Picture
I Can...
use a Capital Letter
The cat is big.
use spaces
sound out words
d-o-g = dog
use a Period .
Draw a picture
The dog and the hog went for a jog but then tripped on a log.
dog
कुत्ता
hog
सूअर
jog
जॉगिंग
log
लकड़ी

Name: ______________________ Date: ______________________

Today is: Monday | Tuesday | Wednesday | Thursday | Friday

Direction: Trace and read the sentences.

bug	hug	jug	mug
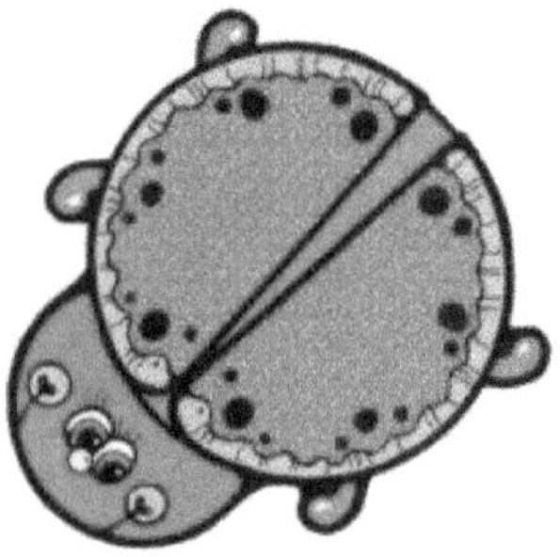			
बग	झप्पी	सुराही	मग

The bug is colorful.

She is hugging.

The jug has milk in it.

He has a mug.

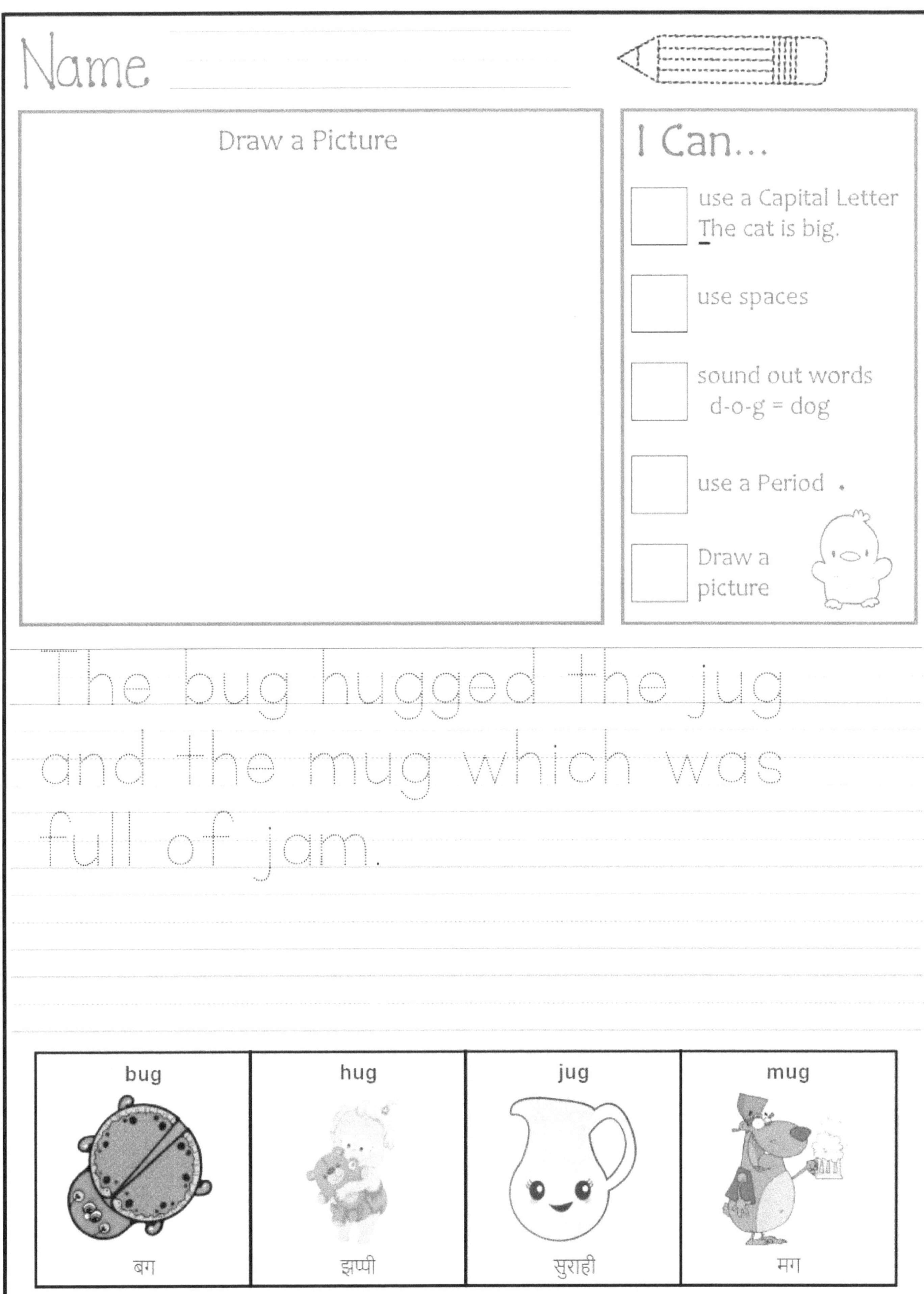

Name
Draw a Picture
I Can...
use a Capital Letter
The cat is big.
use spaces
sound out words
d-o-g = dog
use a Period .
Draw a picture
The bug hugged the jug and the mug which was full of jam.
bug
बग
hug
झप्पी
jug
सुराही
mug
मग

Name: _______________ Date: _______________

Today is: Monday Tuesday Wednesday
Thursday Friday

Direction: Trace and read the sentences.

cot	dot	hot	pot
बिस्तर	डॉट	गरम	मटका

This is my cot.

There are many dots.

It is very hot.

He has a plant pot.

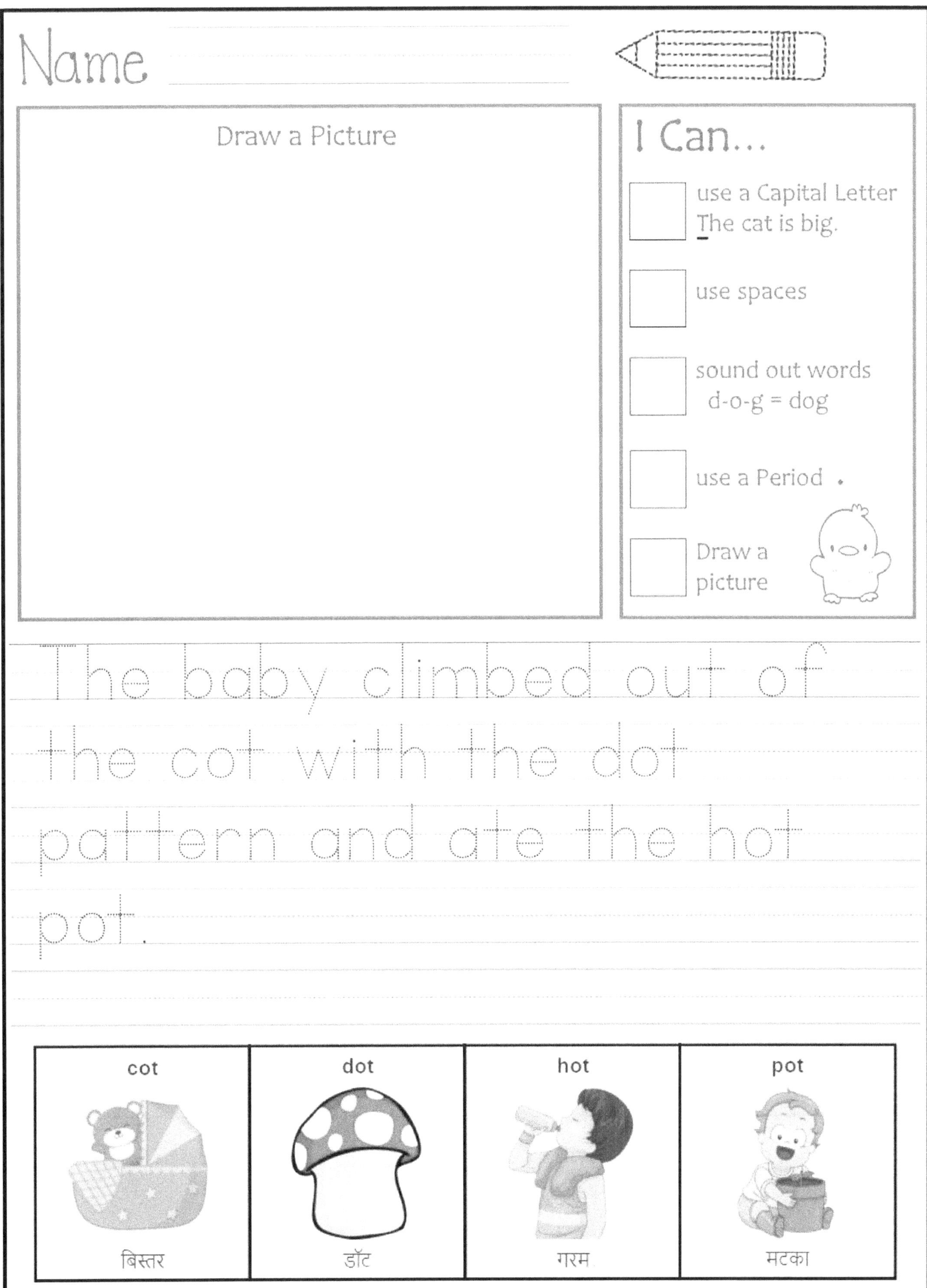

Name

Draw a Picture

I Can...

use a Capital Letter
The cat is big.

use spaces

sound out words
d-o-g = dog

use a Period .

Draw a
picture

The baby climbed out of
the cot with the dot
pattern and ate the hot
pot.

cot
बिस्तर

dot
डॉट

hot
गरम

pot
मटका

Name: ___________________ Date: ___________________

Today is: Monday Tuesday Wednesday Thursday Friday

Direction: Read the words and make a sentence.

fun	gun	run	sun
आनंद	बंदूक	daud	रवि

Name _______________________________

<table>
<tr><td>Draw a Picture</td><td>

I Can...

☐ use a Capital Letter
The cat is big.

☐ use spaces

☐ sound out words
d-o-g = dog

☐ use a Period .

☐ Draw a picture

</td></tr>
</table>

Name: _______________ Date: _______________

Today is: Monday Tuesday Wednesday Thursday Friday

Name: _________________________ Date: _____________

Today is: | Monday | Tuesday | Wednesday |

| Thursday | Friday |

Direction: Read the words and make a sentence.

bag	rag	tag	wag
बैग	खपरैल	टैग	wagging

Name: _______________________

Draw a Picture

I Can...

- [ ] use a Capital Letter
  <u>T</u>he cat is big.

- [ ] use spaces

- [ ] sound out words
  d-o-g = dog

- [ ] use a Period .

- [ ] Draw a picture

Name:

Date:

Today is:

Monday Tuesday Wednesday

Thursday Friday

Name: _________________________ Date: _______________

Today is: | Monday | Tuesday | Wednesday |

| Thursday | Friday |

Direction: Read the words and make a sentence.

| **can** | **man** | **pan** | **van** |
| डिब्बे | आदमी | कड़ाही | वैन |

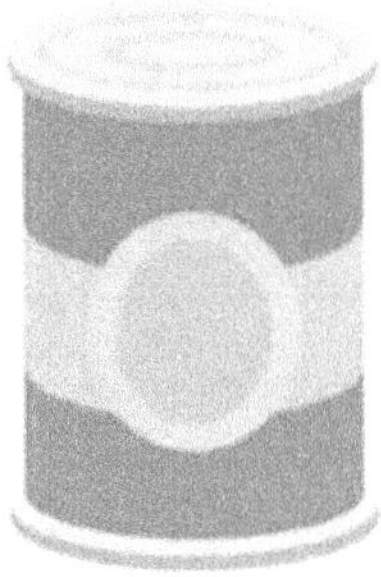

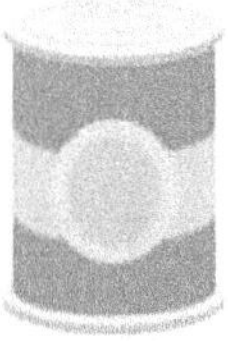

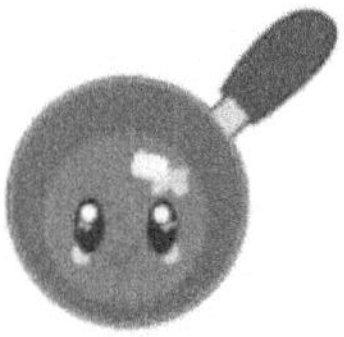

Name _______________________________

Draw a Picture

I Can...

☐ use a Capital Letter
The cat is big.

☐ use spaces

☐ sound out words
d-o-g = dog

☐ use a Period .

☐ Draw a picture

Name: _______________ Date: _______________

Today is: Monday Tuesday Wednesday Thursday Friday

Name: _______________________ Date: _______________

Today is: | Monday | Tuesday | Wednesday |
| Thursday | Friday |

Direction: Read the words and make a sentence.

| cut | gut | hut | nut |
| कट गया | आंत | कुटिया | अखरोट |

Name

Draw a Picture

I Can...

- [ ] use a Capital Letter
  The cat is big.

- [ ] use spaces

- [ ] sound out words
  d-o-g = dog

- [ ] use a Period .

- [ ] Draw a picture

Name: _______________   Date: _______________

Today is: Monday   Tuesday   Wednesday
           Thursday   Friday

Name: _______________________ Date: _______________________

Today is: [Monday] [Tuesday] [Wednesday]
[Thursday] [Friday]

Direction: Read the words and make a sentence.

fat	cat	hat	mat
मोटी	बिल्ली	टोपी	चटाई

Name

Draw a Picture

I Can...

use a Capital Letter
The cat is big.

use spaces

sound out words
d-o-g = dog

use a Period .

Draw a
picture

Name: ___________________ Date: ___________________

Today is: Monday   Tuesday   Wednesday

Thursday   Friday

Name: _______________________ Date: _______________

Today is: | Monday | Tuesday | Wednesday |
           | Thursday | Friday |

Direction: Read the words and make a sentence.

cab	lab	tab	crab
टैक्सी	प्रयोगशाला	टैब	केकड़ा

Name

Draw a Picture

I Can...

use a Capital Letter
The cat is big.

use spaces

sound out words
d-o-g = dog

use a Period .

Draw a
picture

Name: _______________ Date: _______________

Today is: Monday Tuesday Wednesday

Thursday Friday

Name: _________________________ Date: _____________

Today is: Monday Tuesday Wednesday

Thursday Friday

Direction: Read the words and make a sentence.

ham	jam	ram	clam
जांघ	जाम	भेड़	खोल

Name

Draw a Picture

I Can...

- [ ] use a Capital Letter
  The cat is big.

- [ ] use spaces

- [ ] sound out words
  d-o-g = dog

- [ ] use a Period .

- [ ] Draw a picture

Name: _____________________ Date: _____________

Today is: Monday | Tuesday | Wednesday
Thursday | Friday

Name: _______________________ Date: _______________

Today is: Monday   Tuesday   Wednesday
           Thursday   Friday

Direction: Read the words and make a sentence.

bed	led	red	wed
बिस्तर	प्रमुख	लाल	शादी

Name

Draw a Picture

I Can...

- [ ] use a Capital Letter
  The cat is big.

- [ ] use spaces

- [ ] sound out words
  d-o-g = dog

- [ ] use a Period .

- [ ] Draw a picture

Name: ___________________________   Date: ___________________________

Today is:

| Monday | Tuesday | Wednesday |
| Thursday | Friday | |

Name: _________________ Date: _________________

Today is: Monday Tuesday Wednesday

Thursday Friday

Direction: Read the words and make a sentence.

bad	dad	mad	sad
खराब	पिता	पागल	उदास

Name _______________________

<table>
<tr><td>Draw a Picture</td><td>I Can...</td></tr>
</table>

Draw a Picture

I Can...

☐ use a Capital Letter
The cat is big.

☐ use spaces

☐ sound out words
d-o-g = dog

☐ use a Period .

☐ Draw a picture

Name: _______________________ Date: _______________

Today is: Monday Tuesday Wednesday Thursday Friday

Name: ____________________ Date: ____________________

Today is: Monday Tuesday Wednesday Thursday Friday

Direction: Read the words and make a sentence.

den	hen	pen	ten
			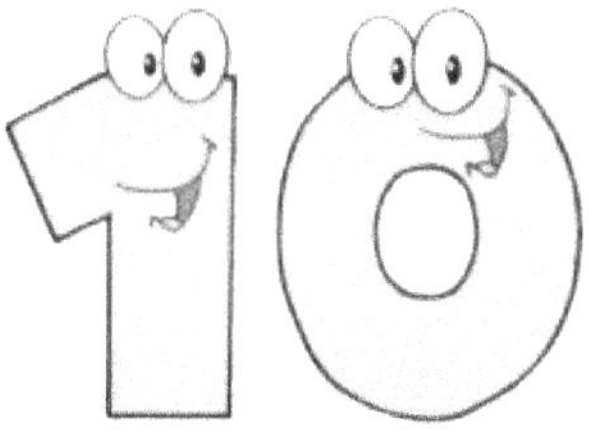
मांद	मुर्गी	अस्तबल	दस

____

____

____

____

Name

Draw a Picture

I Can...

- [ ] use a Capital Letter
  The cat is big.

- [ ] use spaces

- [ ] sound out words
  d-o-g = dog

- [ ] use a Period .

- [ ] Draw a picture

Name: _____________ Date: _____________

Today is: Monday Tuesday Wednesday Thursday Friday

Name: _______________________ Date: _______________

Today is: Monday Tuesday Wednesday Thursday Friday

Direction: Read the words and make a sentence.

gum	mum	sum	drum
चिपचिपा	मां	योग	ड्रम

Name

Draw a Picture

I Can...

- [ ] use a Capital Letter
  The cat is big.

- [ ] use spaces

- [ ] sound out words
  d-o-g = dog

- [ ] use a Period .

- [ ] Draw a picture

Name: _______________________ Date: _______________

Today is: Monday Tuesday Wednesday Thursday Friday

Today is:

Monday	Tuesday	Wednesday

Thursday	Friday

Direction: Read the words and make a sentence.

bid	hid	kid	lid
बोली	छिपाना	बच्चा	ढक्कन

Name

Draw a Picture

I Can...

- [ ] use a Capital Letter
  The cat is big.

- [ ] use spaces

- [ ] sound out words
  d-o-g = dog

- [ ] use a Period .

- [ ] Draw a picture

Name: ___________________   Date: ___________________

Today is: Monday Tuesday Wednesday Thursday Friday

Name: _______________________ Date: _______________________

Today is: Monday | Tuesday | Wednesday
Thursday | Friday

Direction: Read the words and make a sentence.

big	dig	pig	wig
बड़े	गड्ढा करना	सूअर	विग

Name _______________________

Draw a Picture

I Can...

☐ use a Capital Letter
The cat is big.

☐ use spaces

☐ sound out words
d-o-g = dog

☐ use a Period .

☐ Draw a picture

Name: _______________   Date: _______________

Today is: | Monday | Tuesday | Wednesday |
| Thursday | Friday |

Name: _________________   Date: _______________

Today is:

Direction: Read the words and make a sentence.

bin	fin	pin	win
बिन	पंख	पिन	जीत

Name

Draw a Picture

I Can...

- [ ] use a Capital Letter
  The cat is big.

- [ ] use spaces

- [ ] sound out words
  d-o-g = dog

- [ ] use a Period .

- [ ] Draw a picture

Name: Date:

Today is: Monday   Tuesday   Wednesday

Thursday   Friday

Name: _________________________ Date: _______________

Today is: Monday | Tuesday | Wednesday | Thursday | Friday

Direction: Read the words and make a sentence.

hip	lip	nip	sip
कमर	होंठ	चुटकी	पीना

Name ___________________________

<table>
<tr><td>

Draw a Picture

</td><td>

I Can...

☐ use a Capital Letter
The cat is big.

☐ use spaces

☐ sound out words
d-o-g = dog

☐ use a Period .

☐ Draw a picture

</td></tr>
</table>

Name: _______________________ Date: _______________

Today is: Monday Tuesday Wednesday Thursday Friday

Name: _______________________   Date: _______________

Today is: [Monday] [Tuesday] [Wednesday]
           [Thursday] [Friday]

Direction: Read the words and make a sentence.

fit	hit	kit	sit
फिट	मारो	किट	बैठिये

Name

<table>
<tr><td>

Draw a Picture

</td><td>

I Can...

☐ use a Capital Letter
<u>T</u>he cat is big.

☐ use spaces

☐ sound out words
d-o-g = dog

☐ use a Period .

☐ Draw a picture

</td></tr>
</table>

Name: Date:

Today is: Monday   Tuesday   Wednesday

   Thursday   Friday

Name: _________________________ Date: _________________

Today is: Monday Tuesday Wednesday
Thursday Friday

Direction: Read the words and make a sentence.

cob	job	rob	sob
मक्का	काम	लूटना	रोना

Name

Draw a Picture

I Can...

- [ ] use a Capital Letter
  The cat is big.

- [ ] use spaces

- [ ] sound out words
  d-o-g = dog

- [ ] use a Period .

- [ ] Draw a picture

Name: _______________________ Date: _______________________

Today is: Monday Tuesday Wednesday Thursday Friday

Name: _________________________ Date: _______________

Today is: Monday   Tuesday   Wednesday

Thursday   Friday

Direction: Read the words and make a sentence.

dog	hog	jog	log
कुत्ता	सूअर	जॉगिंग	लकड़ी

Name ______________________

<table>
<tr><td>Draw a Picture</td><td>I Can...</td></tr>
</table>

Draw a Picture

I Can...

☐ use a Capital Letter
The cat is big.

☐ use spaces

☐ sound out words
d-o-g = dog

☐ use a Period .

☐ Draw a
picture

Name: ___________________   Date: ___________________

Today is: [Monday] [Tuesday] [Wednesday]
          [Thursday] [Friday]

Name: _____________________ Date: _____________

Today is: [Monday] [Tuesday] [Wednesday]
[Thursday] [Friday]

Direction: Read the words and make a sentence.

bug	hug	jug	mug
बग	झप्पी	सुराही	मग

Name

Draw a Picture

I Can...

- [ ] use a Capital Letter
  The cat is big.

- [ ] use spaces

- [ ] sound out words
  d-o-g = dog

- [ ] use a Period .

- [ ] Draw a picture

Name: ___________________   Date: ___________

Today is: Monday Tuesday Wednesday Thursday Friday

Name: _______________________ Date: _______________________

Today is: | Monday | Tuesday | Wednesday |
| Thursday | Friday |

Direction: Read the words and make a sentence.

cot	dot	hot	pot
बिस्तर	डॉट	गरम	मटका

Name

Draw a Picture

I Can...

- ☐ use a Capital Letter
  <u>T</u>he cat is big.

- ☐ use spaces

- ☐ sound out words
  d-o-g = dog

- ☐ use a Period .

- ☐ Draw a picture

Name: _______________________ Date: _______________________

Today is: Monday Tuesday Wednesday Thursday Friday